D1156037

CELEBRITY BIOS

Jennifer Love Hewitt

Kristin McCracken

St. Margaret Middle School Library
1716-A Churchville Road
Bel Air, Maryland 21015

HIGH
interest
books

Children's Press
A Division of Grolier Publishing
New York / London / Hong Kong / Sydney
Danbury, Connecticut

For Heather, another great role model

Book Design: Nelson Sa
Contributing Editor: Jennifer Ceaser
Photo Credits: Cover © Allen Levenson/Corbis; p. 4 © Corbis; p. 7, © Lisa Rose/Globe Photos Inc.; p. 8 © Grey Vie/Globe Photos Inc.; p. 11 © Globe Photos Inc.; p. 12 © Allen Levenson/Corbis; p. 15 © Albert Sanchez/Atlantic Recording Corporation; p. 16 © Nina Prommer/Globe Photos Inc.; p. 18 © Pacha/Corbis; p. 21 © Nina Prommer/Globe Photos Inc.; p. 23 © Pacha/Corbis; p. 24 © Lisa Rose/Globe Photos Inc.; p. 26 © Henry Mcgee/Globe Photos Inc.; p. 28 © Pacha/Corbis; p. 31 © Alec Michael/Globe Photos Inc.; p. 33 © Lisa Rose/Globe Photos Inc.; p. 35 © Pacha/Corbis; p. 36 © Milan Ryba/Globe Photos Inc.; p. 39 © Lisa Rose/Globe Photos Inc.

Library of Congress Cataloging-in-Publication Data

McCracken, Kristin.
    Jennifer Love Hewitt / by Kristin McCracken.
    p. cm. – (Celebrity bios)
    Includes bibliographical references and index.
    Summary: Examines the life and career of the actress Jennifer Love Hewitt, including her past and present film, television, and singing ventures.
    ISBN 0-516-23321-1 (lib. bdg.) – ISBN 0-516-23521-4 (pbk.)
    1. Hewitt, Jennifer Love, 1979- —Juvenile literature. 2. Actors—United States—Biography—Juvenile literature. [1. Hewitt, Jennifer Love, 1979- 2. Actors and actresses.] I. Title. II. Series.

PN2287.H476 M33 2000
791.43'028'092—dc21
[B]
                                                                00-024228

Copyright © 2000 by Rosen Book Works, Inc.
All rights reserved. Published simultaneously in Canada.
Printed in the United States of America.
1 2 3 4 5 6 7 8 9 10 R 05 04 03 02 01 00

CONTENTS

CHAPTER ONE

Young Love

"I'm a hopeless romantic, so the fact that [Love] is my name is even better."
— Love in *Biography*

It makes sense that Jennifer Love Hewitt prefers to be called Love. It describes the way everyone feels about Jennifer these days: Hollywood producers, her costars, and most of all, her fans around the world. So just how did this small-town Texan become Hollywood's most popular teen queen?

LOVE ARRIVES

Jennifer Love was born in Waco, Texas, on February 21, 1979, to Pat and Danny Hewitt. "Love" was the name of mother Pat Hewitt's

college friend. Both parents thought it perfectly
suited their baby girl.

Jennifer Love grew up in a small Texas town
called Killeen. Her parents divorced when she
was less than a year old. However, Love and her
older brother Todd had a happy childhood with
their mother. Pat Hewitt encouraged her young
daughter's interest in performing. Love started
taking singing and dancing lessons when she was
only three years old. At age six, Love was singing
and dancing in front of large audiences. She
loved the energy of a crowd. Many of Love's
performances were at Texas livestock shows (big
county fairs). The first song she ever sang onstage
was the Whitney Houston hit "The Greatest Love
of All."

Love also was a talented dancer. She knew bal-
let, jazz, and tap. At nine years old, Love joined a
dance group called the Texas Show Team. Love
traveled throughout the Soviet Union and Europe
performing with the dance group.

Love feels very close to her older brother, Todd.

7

Love always knew that she wanted to be an actress.

LOVE GOES TO HOLLYWOOD

Texas may be a big state, but it wasn't big enough for Love. In 1989, Love was ten years old and wanted to go to California and become a real star. Her mother wasn't sure it was a good idea. Finally, a talent agent in Texas convinced Pat that her daughter had what it took to succeed in Hollywood. In an interview with *YM*, Love recalls how badly she wanted to be an actress: "My mom had this little girl who said 'I really, really want to do this crazy thing.' [My mom] basically put her life on hold and moved with my brother and me to California."

It didn't take long for Love to get noticed in Hollywood. In just weeks, she joined the cast of the Disney Channel show "Kids Incorporated." Love sang and danced on the show for two and a half years, from 1989 to 1991. One of her costars was a young actor named Scott Wolf. Little did Love know that four years later, Wolf would be her costar on "Party of Five."

Love also found work in commercials and magazine advertisements. After appearing in several LA Gear ads, Love was hired by the sneaker company to be one of their LA Gear Dancers. She traveled with the dance group, performing in France and Japan.

LOVE RISES

In 1991, twelve-year-old Love appeared in a Barbie exercise video. Not only did Love dance up a sweat, she also sang all of the songs for the workout tape.

The following year, thirteen-year-old Love was cast in a small role in her first movie, *Munchie*. *Munchie* wasn't a big hit. Neither was the 1993 TV movie "Little Miss Millions," in which Love played a young millionaire. One year later, Love snagged a small singing role in the Whoopi Goldberg movie *Sister Act 2: Back in the Habit*.

None of these films made Jennifer Love Hewitt a household name, but she didn't let that

Love wasn't yet a household name, but as a cast member of "Kids Incorporated," she received a Youth in Film Award in 1990.

discourage her. She kept going to auditions, and she was cast in several TV shows. From 1992 to 1994, Love had small roles in the Fox sitcom "Shaky Ground" and in two ABC dramas: "McKenna" and "The Byrds of Paradise."

The "Party of Five" cast, clockwise from top left: Scott Wolf, Matthew Fox, Neve Campbell, Lacey Chabert, and Love Hewitt

Unfortunately, none of these shows were hits, and all of them were cancelled after only a short time. But the failure of these shows turned out to be good news. Love's big break was right around the corner.

In 1995, at age sixteen, Love was cast as Sarah Reeves on the TV show "Party of Five." "Party of Five" was in its second season on Fox. Sarah was supposed to be just a small role. However, audiences liked the character right away. It may have taken Bailey Salinger a while to realize he loved Sarah, but Jennifer Love Hewitt fans—old and new—fell for her right away.

In a 1996 interview with *TV Guide*, Love explained why her character was such a success: "Since 'Party of Five' brought Sarah on, it's been more teen-oriented . . . Sarah's become a huge role model for teenage girls." Yet it wasn't only Sarah Reeves who became a role model. Love herself was becoming the kind of star that teens everywhere could look up to and admire.

LOVE THE SINGER

Believe it or not, Love made music during her rise to acting stardom. She has recorded three albums. In 1992, a teenage Love sang pop music on the album *Love Songs*. She cowrote several songs on her next two albums: 1995's *Let's Go Bang* and the following year's *Jennifer Love Hewitt*.

Love has enjoyed some success as a singer, thanks to her popularity as an actress. However, none of the records have turned her into the next Mariah Carey. For some reason, Love's music never really has caught on with teens in the United States. Yet kids in Japan adore Love's catchy, romantic songs.

Although music is not a priority, Love explains that it is never far from her heart. You can find her song "How Do I Deal" on the soundtrack to *I Know What You Did Last Summer*. Love told *Biography*, "Right now things are so busy with the acting. Singing is something that's very important to me and I don't want to rush into it just for the sake of getting something out there."

Young Love

Love was only sixteen years old when she released
her second album.

CHAPTER TWO

Love in the Movies

"My only mission in life is when I do leave the planet . . . I want to be able to say that everything I wanted to do I did at least once."

—Love in *YM*

Love had become a successful TV actress, but she still wanted to have a movie career. In 1996, during a break in taping "Party of Five," Love acted in the film *House Arrest*. Love played Brooke Figler, a girl who tries to get her parents back together. *House Arrest* didn't break any box office records, but Love enjoyed the chance to work with actress Jamie Lee Curtis. Curtis starred in

Love poses with costar Jamie Lee Curtis at the premiere of *House Arrest*.

I Know What You Did Last Summer starred from left to right: Sarah Michelle Gellar, Ryan Phillipe, Love, and Freddie Prinze, Jr.

many horror movies as a young actress. Little did Love know that she and Curtis soon would have a lot in common.

I KNOW WHAT LOVE DID LAST SUMMER

In the 1990s, horror movies were back in style. Love was eager to follow in the steps of her "Party of Five" costar Neve Campbell. Campbell had become Hollywood's scream queen, thanks to the success of the *Scream* movies. In 1996, Love got her chance.

In *I Know What You Did Last Summer*, Love costarred with some of the hottest young actors in Hollywood: Sarah Michelle Gellar, Freddie Prinze, Jr., and Ryan Phillipe. Love played the character Julie James, a teenager who is terrorized by a killer in a small seaside town.

When *I Know What You Did Last Summer* was released in 1997, it became one of the biggest hits of the summer. It also made Jennifer Love Hewitt one of the biggest teen stars in Hollywood. For her work on the film, Love won a Blockbuster Entertainment Award for Favorite Female Newcomer.

Love found out that it's not easy being a scream queen. During filming, Love had to scream so much, she often lost her voice. During one scene, the director had to think fast because Love couldn't even talk! He had her whisper her lines so they could keep filming.

Sore throat aside, Love told *Teen*, "Making the film was so much fun, a blast acting-wise, a blast mentally, really challenging, and I got to work with incredible people."

LOVE AGAIN

Love had such a good time making *I Know What You Did Last Summer* that she immediately agreed to do the 1998 sequel *I Still Know What You Did Last Summer*. In addition to working with singing sensation Brandy, Love got the chance to work again with Freddie Prinze, Jr.

Love shows off her Blockbuster Entertainment Award.

Did you know?

Love is a talented writer, too. She writes songs, stories, and even film scripts! Her writing was included in the 1997 bestselling book, *Chicken Soup for the Teenage Soul.*

Love did insist, though, that her character develop in the film. She told *YM,* "The one thing I hate about sequels is that the lead character is always the same person. So I made sure Julie was different this time." Love certainly looked different in the hit sequel. She buffed up to play the new and improved Julie by doing a lot of aerobics and weight training.

Love did many of her own stunts while filming the movie. She wound up with more than forty bruises on her body while filming the scenes with the killer. Love sprained her knee, and she also nicked her eye on a piece of metal. Yet Love was rewarded for all her hard work. She won for Favorite Horror Actress at the 1999 Blockbuster Entertainment Awards.

Love shows off her new buffed-up look at the
1998 MTV Video Music Awards.

Love at the premiere of *Can't Hardly Wait*. She earned an MTV
Movie Award nomination for her role in the film.

LOVE IN SCHOOL

In 1998, Love starred in the comedy *Can't Hardly Wait*. She played Amanda Beckett, the most popular girl in high school. The hit film also featured Melissa Joan Hart, Seth Green, and Jerry O'Connell. Love earned an MTV Movie Award nomination for Best Female Performance for her role as Amanda.

Yet Love herself never had a real high school experience as did her character Amanda. In fact, Love was only in high school for six months in Oregon when she was in tenth grade. "I was pretty unpopular," Love recalled during an interview with *Mr. Showbiz*. "I didn't really fit in." She graduated from Laurel Springs High School in 1998 after three years of taking courses through the mail.

MORE TO LOVE

In addition to her blockbuster roles, Love made some smaller films along the way. In the 1997

Love sported bangs soon after she finished filming the role of Audrey Hepburn in the made-for-TV movie.

comedy *Trojan War*, Love starred with then-boyfriend Will Friedle. Love played Leah, a girl who has a crush on her best friend, who happens to be a guy. Leah has to convince her best friend that she's the right girl for him.

In 1998, Love played an ex-girlfriend of a boy she still has feelings for in *Telling You*. The next year, Love acted in the comedy *The Suburbans*. She costarred with Ben Stiller, the star of *There's Something About Mary*. Love played a record executive who wants to help an unpopular band become successful again.

That same year, Love got to live out a dream when she played Audrey Hepburn in a made-for-TV movie. Hepburn, a famous movie actress from the 1950s and '60s, was the star of the popular film *Breakfast at Tiffany's*. Love was excited to film the life of the beautiful actress. She told *Biography*, "Audrey Hepburn has always been my dream role. It was something I never thought I'd be able to do until I was thirty."

CHAPTER THREE

Family, Style, and the Future

"I feel like I'm on this amazing ride, and I just follow my life wherever it's gonna take me."

— Love in Biography

In the fall of 1999, the producers of "Party of Five" decided that Sarah's life was interesting enough to be the basis for a TV show. So Sarah (and Love) left the Salingers behind for a new adventure called "Time of Your Life."

In "Time of Your Life," Sarah moves to New York City in search of her father. It's the story of a brave young woman stepping out on her own,

29

ready to face whatever comes her way. Love feels the same way about her own life. She tells *Teen People,* "Sarah makes this big speech in 'Time of Your Life.' She says she kind of feels like the Marcia Brady of the millennium; maybe she wants to do something daring. I'm kind of like that in my life right now. That doesn't mean I'm going to go out and do anything crazy, but I'm just trying to figure out who I am as a person."

LOVE AND FAMILY

Even though Love is in her early twenties, she still shares a home with her mother (and two cats!) in Los Angeles, California. Pat Hewitt has always supported her daughter's dreams and is proud of Love's many accomplishments. Love explains in a *USA Today* interview, "For my mom, it's not about making me into who she wants me to be. It's about who I am. She tries hard every day to learn what kind of person I'm becoming."

Love regularly appears at many fashionable events. Here she shows off a daring dress at the 1999 Billboard Music Awards.

SERIOUS LOVE

Teens everywhere respect and admire Love. That's why *Teen People* chose her to be on the cover of their very first issue in 1998. The editors understood that Love is a great role model. They even asked her to be part of a team of people who advise the magazine about teen issues.

Love recognizes that the things she says and does influence the way girls think. "I think the best job and the biggest gift I've been given is to be a role model," Love tells *Biography*. "I know that other people say that it's this huge pressure and they don't want it. I know how hard it is to find somebody to look up to. It's such a huge honor and awesome responsibility."

LOVE'S STYLE

Love's fashion sense also has influenced many young teens. As Sarah Reeves, Love made long, straight, dark hair popular. Soon, actresses, models, and people everywhere copied Love's look.

Love attends the launch party for *Teen People*, a magazine for which she advises about teen issues.

For her clothing, Love prefers her own original fashion sense. She likes to mix different styles together. "Some days, I want to put on a long, flowy sundress and feel girlie," Love tells *Teen People*. "Other times, I wake up and want to be an Abercrombie & Fitch girl."

LOVE AND HER CAREER

Not content with just being an actress, Love recently took a big step. She created her own film production company called Love Spell Productions. Having her own company means that she will have more say about the kinds of projects on which she works.

So far, Love has developed a script for a movie about a wedding planner who falls in love with the groom. The story for the film grew out of a dream Love had one night. "It was so nice, I just wanted to share it with people. But I never thought anything would happen with it," she told *Mr. Showbiz*. She told some of her friends about

Love looks glamorous at the recent Golden Globe Awards.

Love always makes time for charity work. Here, she helps to dish out meals at a Thanksgiving dinner for the homeless.

her idea for the script. They encouraged her to do something about it. So Love dressed up in a suit, marched into the movie studio New Line Cinema, and said, "Forget I'm an actress and just let me tell you the story and see if you like it." The studio liked the idea so much, they even asked Love to star in the film!

Love's future projects include the film *Breakers* and another movie called *Bunny*. Love also will be the voice of Thumbelina in the animated movie *The Adventures of Tom Thumb and Thumbelina*.

LOVE AND CHARITY

No matter how busy she is, Love always finds time to spend on charity work. One of her favorite causes is Big Sisters/Little Sisters, an organization in which women offer to spend time and develop relationships with needy children. She also is involved with Tuesday's Child, which helps children who have HIV/AIDS.

LUCKY IN LOVE?

Love has had several high-profile boyfriends over the years. Her first date, at age fourteen, was with Fred Savage, star of "The Wonder Years." In 1996, Love briefly dated Joey Lawrence (of "Blossom"). One year later, she started a long relationship with "Boy Meets World" star Will Friedle. She dated MTV veejay Carson Daly, with whom she broke up in September 1999. Love also has been linked to Rich Cronin from the group LFO. Love told *USA Weekend*: "Apparently, I'm dating eighty-five different people at once. I'm exhausted from the love life that [the press has] given me. There is [a guy], but it's minimal. And I've learned not to talk about it."

LOVE AND THE FUTURE

What's in store for the young actress? Love's not even sure herself. In an interview with *Mr. Showbiz*, Love said, "I've always wanted to go to college. I'll go one day. The great thing about

Love gets a hug from former boyfriend Carson Daly.

college is it's never too late or too early to go.
But I will have that college experience someday."

Jennifer Love Hewitt has the talent and the
ambition to keep her at the top. Whether Love
is acting, singing, or modeling, her personality,
beauty, and warmth shine through.

TIMELINE

1979
- Jennifer Love Hewitt is born in Texas.

1989
- Love and her mother move to Los Angeles, California.
- Love joins the cast of "Kids Incorporated."
- Love is hired as a dancer for LA Gear.

1991
- Love stars in a Barbie exercise video.

1992
- Love's first album, *Love Songs,* is released in Japan.
- *Munchie* is released.

1993
- The TV movie "Little Miss Millions" airs.
- The sitcom "Shaky Ground" debuts on the Fox network and is soon canceled.
- Love has a small role in *Sister Act 2: Back in the Habit.*

1994
- The television drama "Byrds of Paradise" is on for one season.
- Love joins the cast of TV's "McKenna."

1995	• Love's character Sarah Reeves is added to the cast of "Party of Five."
	• Love releases her second album, *Let's Go Bang*.
1996	• *House Arrest* is released.
	• Love records her third album, *Jennifer Love Hewitt*.
1997	• *Trojan War* is released.
	• *I Know What You Did Last Summer* hits theaters in the summer.
	• Love receives a nomination for Best Actress in a Television Drama Series for her role as Sarah Reeves on "Party of Five."
1998	• *I Still Know What You Did Last Summer* comes out in theaters.
	• *Telling You* is released in video stores.
	• *Can't Hardly Wait* comes out in theaters.
	• Love wins a Blockbuster Entertainment Award for Favorite Female Newcomer for her role as Julie in *I Know What You Did Last Summer*.

TIMELINE

1999
- *The Suburbans* is released.
- Love announces she's leaving "Party of Five."
- "Time of Your Life" debuts on Fox.
- Love earns two Teen Choice Awards: Female Hottie of the Year and Choice Movie Actress of the Year.
- Love wins a Blockbuster Entertainment Award for Favorite Actress in a Horror Film for *I Still Know What You Did Last Summer.*
- Love appears in the LFO music video "Girl on TV."

2000
- The ABC-TV movie about Audrey Hepburn's life airs in March.
- Love wins the People's Choice Award for Favorite Performer in a New TV Series for "Time of Your Life."

FACT SHEET

Name	Jennifer Love Hewitt
Nickname	Love
Birthdate	February 21, 1979
Birthplace	Waco, Texas
Family	One brother, Todd; mother, Pat; father, Danny
Sign	Pisces
Hair	auburn brown
Eyes	hazel brown
Height	5' 2"

Favorites

Actor	Johnny Depp
Actresses	Audrey Hepburn, Natalie Wood
Movies	*Sixteen Candles, Don Juan DeMarco, Breakfast at Tiffany's*
TV Shows	"South Park," "Friends," "Frasier," "Seinfeld"
Foods	strawberries, McDonald's Happy Meals, mushroom pizza
Bands	Matchbox 20, Third Eye Blind, Green Day
Singers	Shawn Colvin, Aretha Franklin, Sarah McLachlan
Pets	Two cats: Don Juan DeMarco and Haylie
Hobbies	karaoke, collecting angels
Sports	(doing) rollerblading, surfing, hiking (watching) hockey, football, boxing

NEW WORDS

aerobics a form of exercise that involves an increased heart rate

audition a try-out performance in hopes of getting a role in a movie or TV show

costar a person who stars in a film or TV show alongside another star

drama hour-long television show

Hollywood area in California where most movies and TV shows are done

livestock shows big county fairs that include rodeos and musical performances

movie studio a company that gives the money to a director to make a film

nomination selection of someone for an award

producer the person who supervises the production of a record, film, or TV show

production company a company that makes films and TV shows

record executive a person who finds new musical talent

role a character or part played by a performer in a movie or TV show

script the actual lines characters say in a movie or TV show

season a specific period of the year when a television series airs

sequel follow-up to a movie

sitcom television comedy show, usually thirty minutes in length

soundtrack the music recorded for a movie

FOR FURTHER READING

Aronson, Virginia. *Jennifer Love Hewitt* (Galaxy of Superstars). Broomall, PA: Chelsea House Publishers, 1999.

Golden, Anna Louise. *Jennifer Love Hewitt*. New York: Saint Martin's Press, 1999.

Hewitt, Jennifer Love, Brandy and Robert Moritz. *On Location With Love and Brandy: A Behind the Scenes Diary of* I Still Know What You Did Last Summer. New York: Archway Paperbacks, 1998.

Murphy, Catherine Frey. *Jennifer Love Hewitt*. Kansas City, MO: Andrews & McMeel, 1999.

RESOURCES

WEB SITES

Internet Movie Database—Jennifer Love Hewitt
www.us.imdb.com/Name?Hewitt,+Jennifer+Love
Jennifer Love Hewitt's Internet Movie Database
page. It includes information about her movies,
TV shows, and music. It also includes a short
biography of the actress.

Time of Your Life
www.Fox.com/timeofyourlife
The official Web site for "Time of Your Life,"
with episode guides and interviews with the cast.

You can write to Love at the folllowing address:

Jennifer Love Hewitt
c/o "Time of Your Life"
FOX Broadcasting Company
10201 W. Pico Boulevard
Los Angeles, CA 90035

INDEX

ABOUT THE AUTHOR

Kristin McCracken is an educator and writer living in New York City. Her favorite activities include seeing movies, plays, and the occasional star on the street.